Inside Attica:
Riot To Revival

**The True Story of Attica Prison's
Unlikely Chaplain**

Inside Attica:
Riot To Revival

The True Story of Attica Prison's Unlikely Chaplain

Rob Wright

𝓅

S.E.L.F. PUBLISHING
Simple, Effective, Literary Focusing on Publishing

INSIDE ATTICA, RIOT TO REVIVAL
COPYRIGHT © 2009 By ROB WRIGHT

Book & Cover Design By David Chapman
www.yourvisualimage.com

℘

S.E.L.F. PUBLISHING
4075 S Durango Dr.
Suite 111 #220
Las Vegas, NV 89147
Visit us at www.yourpublisher.org

All rights reserved. This material is protected under the copyright laws and may not be copied or reprinted. No portion of this book may be reproduced in any form or by any means, electronic, mechanical, photocopying, recording or otherwise without the written permission of the publisher.

Unless otherwise noted, Scripture was taken from the Holy Bible, New International Version®. NIV®. Copyright © 1973, 1978, 1984, by International Bible Society used by permission of Zondervan. All rights reserved.

First Edition, March	1984		Fourth, October	1985
Second, August	1984		Fifth, December	1986
Third, March	1985		Sixth Edition, June	2009

ISBN # 0-9776335-9-4

Printed & Bound by Publishers' Graphics, LLC

Printed In The United States Of America

CONTENTS

Open Doors……………………………………….. 14
Moving Up……………………………………….... 22
A Growing Work…………………………………. 28
An Unlikely Chaplain…………………….. 32
A Matter of Color…………………………………. 47
The Ministry Grows………………………..... 55
The Story of Steve………………………………… 59
The Bum Story…………………………………..... 65
An Invitation to Africa…………………… 75
Saying Good-Bye…………………………… 89
Addendum…………………………………….... 94
Plan of Salvation………………………………….. 96

DEDICATION

This book is dedicated to all those who labor in the prison ministry, those unsung heroes of the faith that bring hope to the hopeless.

I have attempted to share this story without preaching, as I believe this testimony of God's faithfulness can speak for itself.

Although I originally wrote this book over twenty-four years ago, I know that this story of God's love and mercy will be an encouragement to all those who will read it.

This is the sixth printing of this book, the last one being December 1986. I thought it would never be printed again, but the Lord had other ideas.

I would like to thank the precious folks at Abundant Grace Church in Las Vegas, Nevada, where I now pastor. Through their gifts and their love they encouraged me in this project.

I would also like to thank my wife Julie for her tireless efforts in correcting my grammar, and my son David who designed the new cover for the book.

Rob Wright

PROLOGUE

His nickname is "The Ox." The Ox has the distinction of being the strongest man in the entire Attica State Prison. He was serving two life terms and is noted for his meanness and brute strength. His heavily-muscled black body was a result of hours of weight lifting and training in the prison weight rooms. I knew from his background that he had the respect of every man in the prison. I found out that at one time he hit a man so hard in the jaw that it snapped the man's collar bone. In a loud, boisterous voice he shouted, "Preacher, come over here!" As I walked over, he looked at me; and with a smirk on his face announced that the word was out throughout the prison, "They are going to kill you. Someone has made a knife in the metal shop and they are going to stick you with it during the services." As I heard these words my heart sank even more. Now it was apparent; it was my time to face death.

"Then the righteous will answer him, 'Lord, when did we see you hungry and feed you, or thirsty and give you something to drink? When did we see you a stranger and invite you in, or needing clothes and clothe you? When did we see you sick or in prison and go to visit you?
The King will reply, 'I tell you the truth, whatever you did for one of the least of these brothers of mine, you did for me."

                                            Jesus
                                     Matthew 25:37-40

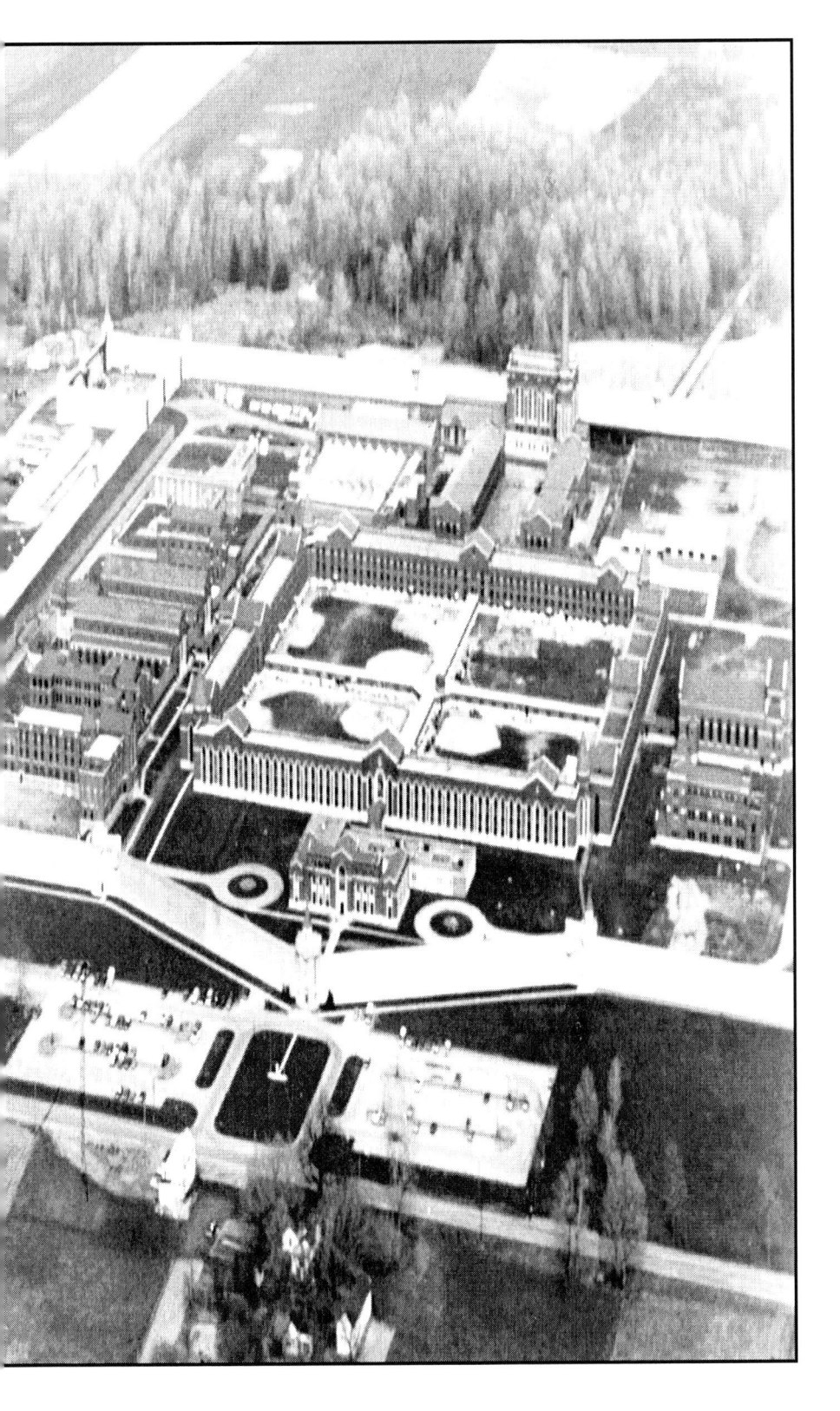

OPEN DOORS

The windshield wiper on my old Plymouth beat a steady staccato as I drove the back roads of western New York heading towards the county seat in Albion, New York. I was driving to the county jail to hold a service or to make arrangements to make visits. I had never been to this jail before, but while praying with a pastor friend, the Lord had given us a special scripture. That scripture was Revelation 3:8 "I know your deeds. See, I have placed before you an open door that no one can shut. I know that you have little strength, yet you have kept my word and have not denied my name". It was an exciting time as I drove. The wet, heavy snow of the western New York winter could not hinder my great expectations, as I knew God would be opening doors.

As I drove, I reflected on how God had changed my life up to this time. Growing up in a religious home, I rebelled by going into the Navy and serving three tours in Vietnam as a combat air-crewman. After having a life-changing experience with the Lord, I knew I was called into the ministry. A short time after coming home, I studied for the ministry while working as a deputy sheriff. With my size and experience in the military, it was only natural for me to work in some type of law enforcement. It was while I worked as a deputy sheriff that God revealed to me His great love for those in prison. God had a plan and purpose for my life.

I had been assigned to a work detail taking twelve inmates from the local jail in western New York out to a local county park to cut trees and move brush. It was like a chain-gang, but no one had any chains. Most of these men were just serving jail time for small crimes. These were not hardened criminals, just men who had made some bad judgments.

In New York, men could serve one year in jail, and for more serious crimes were sentenced to a correctional facility (prison). It was while I was with these men that the Lord began to speak to me their great need for Christ. It had been hard for me to make the first move. Every day the three deputies and I stood and watched these men for eight hours with loaded weapons as they cleared brush. Every day at noon we would load them into the truck while they ate their noon-day meal. It was a strict, disciplined time. We didn't converse with the inmates. They were on one side of the fence and we were on the other side. But God had a plan, not only for the inmates, but also for me.

It was during this time that God began to speak to me and show me in His scriptures how he had changed my life dramatically several years before and had filled me with His Holy Spirit. I had been changed into a new man, and now God was telling me that I was to share this message with the inmates. I wrestled greatly with this situation until one day at noon hour as the men were sitting in the truck, I took off my weapons, got into the back of the truck and began to share what Christ had done in my life: how He had changed me and given me new hope, how He had healed me, mentally and physically in so many ways.

I thought at first the men would laugh. They did not know that I was a Christian; they didn't know anything about me. I was the authority. I was the one that drove the truck and guarded them daily. I began to speak, and as I did, tears came to my eyes. I carried my New Testament and began to share with them the great victory we can have as Christians. To my surprise, no one laughed, no one mocked me; and as I asked the men to pray, six of them asked Jesus Christ to be their personal Savior. That night in the locker room, as we were preparing to change our clothes, the deputy that was working with me approached me and expressed a need for Christ, as well. It was at that time that God began to show me the special anointing I would have for those in prison.

Through changes in the sheriff's department, I no longer had my job, but had been called into full-time ministry. After praying and seeking the advice of several pastors, it was truly the Lord that was leading me to Albion, New York, to go into this prison situation and test the waters. It was with great anticipation that I drove those back roads, and as I pulled into Albion, I checked my directions one more time to find the location of the county jail. According to the directions, I couldn't miss it. It was in the center of a square entitled "Church Square"; and as I drove up, I could see the reason why. Eight churches surrounded this three-story facility. I knew it was a jail immediately because of the barred windows and the police cars outside the building. It had the look of an official government institution. I looked again as I parked the car, to the churches around the square. There were eight churches of all different denominations, and their steeples and crosses dwarfed the jail building. As I walked up the front steps, I thought surely they must have many services inside this facility. There must be full-time chaplains and lots of Bibles, and surely there would be a chance for me to begin in a new direction. I opened the front doors and walked in, and to the right I saw a large metal door. As I approached the door, I pushed the button to ring for an officer; and a small heavy-set man with a "brush-cut" came forward. He was very stern and official-looking. His shoes were highly polished, his badge shined, and his shirt was military-pressed. He looked to be someone of great authority. He said,

"Could I help you sir?" With great anticipation I stuttered and stammered and was finally able to say, "Yes, my name is Reverend Wright, and I am here to make myself available to perform a chapel service." A smirk turned the corners of his mouth upward; he eyed me from the top of my head to my toes. He looked again at the Bible I was carrying and he said, "Preacher, we don't have Bibles here. We don't have ministers here. We don't have a chapel here, and we don't need one." With that he turned on his heels, walked through the door, and the metal door slammed in my face. I stood there completely in shock. God had given me Revelation 3:8, "See, I have placed before you an open door that no one can shut," but by all appearances the door had been closed in my face.

It was with great embarrassment now that I felt I would have to drive back home. Had I missed God? Had I listened to voices that were not God's? Had I moved out on my own instead of being obedient to God? I sat in the chair in the waiting room. It was a very bleak, governmental-looking waiting room with two chairs, an ashtray, and a picture of our president. Not knowing what to do, I simply sat and began to pray. I prayed for a matter of minutes, when a man put his hand on my shoulder. I looked up to see a well-dressed man in a business suit, a gentle face, and a warm smile. He said, "Can I help you, sir? What's wrong?" I didn't know the man; I knew nothing about him, but his smile gave me indication that he cared. I poured my heart out to the man and shared with him the frustration I had felt. I shared my experiences as a deputy sheriff, how Christ had changed my life, how God had given me the scripture Revelation 3:8, and how I felt the Lord was leading me to work in the prison ministry, and to begin by coming here to Albion. He looked at me very intently and said to me, "Follow me." As he walked up to the door, the door opened, and the official-looking officer came to attention. He said to the man, "Take Reverend Wright and prepare for him an I.D. Card." The man, who I later found out to be the Warden, said, "What should I put on it, Sheriff?" The Sheriff said, "You put on it, Protestant Chaplain." Surely, God had opened the doors. The Sheriff, Don White, had served as the sheriff in that county for sixteen years. With him we were able to establish a chapel with services, and God moved in a mighty way. Truly God was leading in opening doors, and we were following.

Later, Sheriff Don White was on our radio broadcast sharing how he had accepted Jesus Christ as his personal Savior. In the time that I served at the jail, many men found Christ, both inmates and deputies; and God was truly opening doors that no man could close.

MOVING UP

The jail ministry is a difficult ministry because many of the men are only in the jail for a short period of time awaiting sentencing. In New York State, the maximum time a man can spend in a local jail is one year. If he is sentenced to a longer amount of time, he is sent to either a minimum or maximum security prison. The difference depends on the seriousness of his crime. Many of the men that I had ministered to in the Albion jail were being sentenced to serve their time in the maximum security prison at Attica.

Soon I began to receive letters from men who had found Christ and had been transferred to Attica. In their letters they spoke of a need for Christian fellowship. They had looked for a Bible study and many of the things they were used to in the Albion County jail, but were unable to find them in a large maximum security prison. Soon they wrote with requests for Bibles and for visits. I knew it was time for me to make my first trip to Attica Prison.

The prison is located in the small community of Attica, New York. It was a drive of approximately an hour and a half from my home. As I approached the small town I could see the evidences of a prison nearby. Many of the men that I saw on the streets, passing through town, had their uniforms on and were either coming to the prison or leaving the prison to head for home. Attica Prison is a large maximum security facility which employs 490 full-time prison guards. This is not counting the many staff people and teachers that also work within the walls. Attica Prison is 113 acres within the thirty-five foot walls, and most men never go any further than these huge walls. There is a farm, but it is maintained only by trustees. As I drove over the hill to see the prison, it was overwhelming. There, like some gigantic medieval fortress, it stood. The grey, cold walls, the gun towers, the fences were all eerie in appearance. I parked my car and walked to the front gate. I had the names of several of the men I was going to visit, and as I prepared to visit the men, I saw for the first time the effect of serving time on prisoners' families. There in the waiting room, like so many cattle, were the families: mothers, fathers, wives, and children of the eighteen hundred inmates serving time in this maximum security prison. I sat there feeling out of place, but my concern for the men far outweighed my fears. These men needed a visit. They needed Christian fellowship. I knew that God had blessed me before in opening doors, and I believed He would this time.

After filling out the proper paper work, I went through the metal detector, emptied my pockets, and was ushered into the prison waiting room. There in the waiting room men are allowed to sit across the table from their loved ones. They are allowed one kiss as they come in and one kiss as they leave. On both ends of the room sat guards that watch every move; and except for an occasional trip to a vending machine, there was very little unnecessary movement. That day I visited two men. I spent approximately two hours with one man and three with the next. There was a great time of fellowship and reunion as we shared what Christ was doing in our lives. I had carried my Bible and shared scriptures with the men, and I felt greatly encouraged as I left that day. One of the men I had seen asked me to pray about coming in and teaching a Bible study. I shared with him that I knew no one in the prison and that I had no connections in the prison authority. Attica was a state prison; and I had little, if any, of the necessary requirements to teach a Bible study there.

It was about two months later that I received a phone call one night from a pastor in the Attica area. He had heard that I would be interested in teaching the Thursday night Bible study inside the prison. When I responded with a LOUD "Praise the Lord," he was quick to tell me that I may be getting into more than I could handle. He shared the great discouragement he had felt in dealing with men that were unable to respect him. He painted a grim picture of uncaring, unloving, mean men with little or no education and no desire to learn. It was later that I found out that he had been preaching from the Old

Testament on the laws and regulations. I knew that God had called me to preach the love of Jesus. As we made arrangements on the phone, I prepared myself for the first visit to Thursday night Bible study.

    The first Thursday night I arrived at the prison, it was quite a different site at night with all the lights. There, standing like some gigantic light-house, was Attica Prison. Its lights shone all over the prison and up the huge walls. There were thirteen gates and electric doors that I had to pass through on my way to the classrooms where the Bible study was held. As I walked down those long corridors, I thought, "How do I approach these men, God?" In the natural, it seems very unlikely that an ex-deputy sheriff would be able to relate to men in prison. I asked the Lord again in my spirit the question, "God, how do I minister to these men?" The still small voice inside me said, "Love them as I loved you." I had found in my experience as a prison minister that it was the love of Jesus that changed people. The men knew that they had committed crimes. They knew they were sinners, but it was the compassionate, caring, forgiving love of Jesus that caused them to change from crime to

Christ. I shared my testimony and told them of the love of Jesus. I found them to be a responsive, loving group of men. They were hungry for love and hungry for the things of God. I left that night knowing again that God had opened another door.

A GROWING WORK

The Bible study on Thursday nights had grown to about one hundred men. I was involving business men from the Buffalo area who were Christians and wanted to be involved in the prison ministry. The men from Buffalo would meet me at the gate on Thursday nights and come in and sit and share with the inmates. When men in prison hear successful business men talk about Jesus and how he has blessed them, they respond much quicker than they would for a preacher that they know will talk about Jesus. Growth occurred on both sides. The men in prison grew strong in the Lord. The men who came in from the outside grew as they testified to the glory of God, and the ministry began to blossom in a way that it never had before.

We had moved out of the classroom and into

the hall because of lack of space. Our loud singing and praising bothered many who were taking other classes, and complaints were coming in steadily from the other classrooms. One day I received a phone call from the prison chaplain asking if it would be alright if we moved to the locker room adjacent to the gym. I said it would be fine with me, and the following Thursday we met in the locker room.

The ministry grew stronger and there were new men every week. The testimony of how Christ could change men's lives had been witnessed throughout the entire prison. From time to time, we also brought in visiting ministers and singers to minister to the men. These were great times in Christian fellowship. The bond that was created between these men and myself was one I will never forget. The love they showed to me, the sharing, the sincere ministry one to another, is unforgettable. We began to pray for the needs of the men, and God began to pour out His Spirit in a mighty way. The sight of over one hundred men raising their hands in praise to the Lord is truly awesome. The resounding voices, as they sang praises to God, could be heard throughout that entire section of the prison. The Thursday night Bible study became the talk of the entire institution. Because of space, there were men on waiting lists that were unable to attend.

At that time, we felt it was best to move into the auditorium. On the night we moved into the auditorium, over 175 men came to Thursday night Bible study. It was a time of sharing, singing, and special ministry as we prayed for the sick and those with special needs. God was establishing a church inside those prison walls. It was truly an exciting time.

One night a man had a special request. He felt that God had impressed on him that we should write on the chalkboard the names of those people who needed special prayer. I had expected the names of loved ones and family, but to my surprise the men began to call out the names of guards and those in authority. Even the name of the warden of the prison was called out. It was a moving sight as the men laid hands on the chalkboard and we prayed for those names. Truly the Spirit of the Lord was in that prison that night.

The response from the outside visitors had

grown to such an extent that now I could only allow a few to visit with me on each night. Following the service in the prison, we would go to a local restaurant in Batavia, New York and share for hours of the good fellowship we had received in the prison.

At this time, I was serving full-time in the prison ministry. Besides the Thursday night Bible study, I was also traveling to churches and different groups on weekends to share the good news of men's lives being changed behind prison bars. Our radio broadcast, "From the Chaplain's Desk," was being aired on six different stations weekly. We were sending Bibles to every man who requested one from all over the eastern United States. My series of five Bible studies was being sent to many different men and women in jails and institutions across the country. I was seeing the fulfillment of Revelation 3:8 in my life. My mailing list had grown to a large number. I knew surely that God had called me into prison ministry. It was exciting to share the prison ministry, not only in full-gospel churches, but in all denominations. I was living in Byron, New York, a suburb of Rochester. Little did I know what the Lord had ahead for me in the future.

AN UNLIKELY CHAPLAIN

What happened next is something that, still to this day, I cannot understand. Although I have shared this part of the story all over the United States from coast to coast, it still amazes me how God can be so sovereign. On one particular Thursday night before the service, one of the men mentioned to me that a group of men had formed and were praying that I would become the Protestant Chaplain. I really didn't pay much attention to this statement because the prison already had a Protestant Chaplain who was appointed by the state of New York. He was an elderly man whose wife was very sick and, because of this, his attendance at the prison had suffered. He also found the charismatic type of worship and the evangelical style of preaching very different to the training that he had. I had been teaching the Bible study at this time for approximately two years. During this time, I seldom, if ever, saw the chaplain. I usually communicated with his office through his secretary, or the few times that I did talk to him was over the phone. I knew he was very concerned for his wife and he felt very drawn to her at this time.

On the following Thursday night the men again mentioned that they were praying that I would become the chaplain. I knew enough about prison chaplaincy and the New York State requirements to know that I did not have the necessary qualifications. There are several advanced degrees that are necessary; there is preclinical training that is needed, and most of the chaplains in the state of New York come from mainline denominations. I knew that there was no way that I could become their chaplain. I became very concerned for them, as I felt that their unanswered prayer could lead to serious doubt.

On the following Thursday night, the men again mentioned that they were still praying. They had formed a prayer clock, whereby they took a chalkboard and sectioned it into half-hour segments, so that the twenty-four hours were covered completely in prayer. The focus of that prayer was that I would become the Protestant Chaplain. Still to this day, I find it utterly amazing the ability of men behind prison walls to intercede around the clock for me to become their chaplain. The night they shared that with me, I became angry. I said, "Men, I can't become your chaplain. You don't seem to understand that I don't have the necessary requirements. I come from the wrong background. I don't have the education or the ecclesiastical requirements." After I finished sharing this, one big Puerto Rican man in the back of the room stood to his feet and challenged me. He said, "Brother Rob, you preach faith, you teach us faith, but you don't have the faith to believe God yourself to become the chaplain." As he spoke these words, they pierced my heart. I knew that I, in fact, did not have the faith that they had. How many times in the prison ministry had I found men, once converted, walking in childlike faith, able to believe God, but many people on the outside were not able to? That night, I asked the men to lay hands on me and pray that God would increase my faith. I knew in that moment that God was going to allow me to become the chaplain of that prison. I didn't know how or when, but I knew that the anointing of God was on those men as they prayed for me.

It was the following day, on a Friday, that I received a phone call from the State Capitol in Albany and spoke to a Reverend Doctor Earl Moore, who, at that time, was the Director of Chaplaincy in the New York State Department of Corrections. He asked me if I could fill in as a contract chaplain on Sunday mornings until they could find someone more qualified. I remember the joy that filled my heart, the excitement I felt as I prepared for the first Sunday morning service. What a joy it would be to share with the men how their prayers had been answered!

That Sunday morning, I went into the auditorium where the Sunday services are held, and waited as the Catholic service was conducted and then the men were called out for the Protestant service. As the Catholic men filed out, I waited with great anticipation to see my Christian brothers and to share with them God's faithfulness in answering prayer.

AN UNLIKELY CHAPLAIN

I was surprised to see the men file in. They were men that I had never seen before. They were dressed in a way that I had never seen before. I found out later that Attica Prison, because it is divided into four different sections, is like four different prisons in one. Many men will never see another inmate during their whole prison term. The only time they can see the other men would be on Sunday morning when men of all four sections are allowed to come to Sunday morning interdenominational services. What happened, very frankly, was that the homosexual men had taken over the Sunday morning worship service.

Because of sickness in the family, the Protestant chaplain was not there much of the time. Because of the different problems he was facing, many services went unattended.

Very honestly, what happened was that the homosexual faction inside the prison had made Sunday morning their meeting place. I saw men dressed in a manner that I had never seen before. Some of them had bloused their shirts into a form that would make them effeminate. Some of the men had on makeup. In one area of the congregation, there were men trading magazines out of paper bags. The pornography was unlike any I had ever seen, and there on Sunday morning it had taken on the air of a flea market whereby men could trade their smut with other men. Another group of men were smoking. I noticed that some men actually held hands and fondled one another as they came in. I had never seen anything like this. It was beyond my comprehension.

Homosexuality in prison is a matter of life. The men who are homosexual are not the effeminate type that one would expect. They are strong, militant men who have taken an alternative lifestyle to fulfill their sexual needs.

I came to the place that morning where I knew I had to stand for the Gospel of Jesus Christ. I looked out into the congregation of almost 300 men and didn't see any of my Christian friends. I never had the chance to tell them that I would be there Sunday morning. I had taken for granted that they would be there, but I soon found out that the Thursday night Bible study had become their church. What was at one time a Protestant service had become a mockery. It was nothing more than a meeting place for those who wished to do as they pleased. I stepped to the microphone but everyone just continued what they were doing. I began to shout, but to no avail. Finally, I went to the amplifier and turned it up to the level whereby it squealed. The men began to look. Looks of indignation and anger came over their faces. I turned the microphone down to an audible level and spoke with boldness, "Men, my name is Reverend Wright and I am your new chaplain. When you come to services from now on you will not be dressed like girls; you will not bring dirty magazines; you will not smoke cigarettes; you will come in a manner that will glorify God. When we stand up to sing, you will sing, and when we bow our heads to pray, you are all going to pray. And from now on the bathroom will be locked during services." The reason that I decided to lock the bathrooms was that I had noticed the men going there two at a time, undoubtedly to perform homosexual acts. The guards looked at me strangely as well. For weeks now, they had allowed the inmates to do as they pleased during this one hour time, and found it easier to allow them to do as they wished than to try to make them have some kind of service.

The response to my introduction was far from cordial.

Following the service, three of the men came to the corner of the auditorium and began pushing and shoving me. Their loud words and cursing scared me. They had something good going and they didn't want it changed. They told me that if I came back to the prison, they would kill me. I knew the intent of the men's hearts. Finally the guards pulled them off me, and they were taken back to their cells.

As I left the prison that day, I felt a fear similar to the fear I felt while serving in Vietnam. I knew that my life was in jeopardy. I even questioned my calling. I wondered if God had really called me to be the chaplain, and if he truly called me, would he allow these men to kill me?

All over Western New York, churches and prayer groups of all denominations began to pray for me. I received calls from people that I didn't know encouraging me to stand. That week was one of prayer and fasting. My precious mother, Marjorie, was a constant encouragement to me. Her deep faith in God always amazed me. She had prayed for me when I was lost and running from God, and always said that God told her that I would be a "man of God" one day. She was a true "prayer warrior." I'm blessed to say that I am a product of a praying, godly mother.

The following Sunday morning, I awoke early and prayed. The drive to the prison that morning was a long one, filled with prayer, filled with praise, filled with the confession that, "No, in all these things we are more than conquerors through Him who loved us." (Romans 8:37). As I drove, I remembered that I had not prepared a sermon. I was so concerned with praying for my life that I didn't get a message together. I had some time before the service began, so I went to the chaplain's office and dropped to my knees. After I prayed, I felt that the Lord was impressing me to preach on Jesus clearing the temple of the money changers (Mark 11:15). Jesus said, "My house shall be called a house of prayer." I asked the Lord, "Father, can't I speak on brotherhood, or love, or reverence, or fellowship?" But again, I felt the impression; I must preach what the Spirit commanded.

I began to walk to the auditorium area. As I share this story, I tell many people that my knees were "having fellowship," because of the great fear that tried to overtake me. I knew without a doubt that these men were capable of killing me. Since there is no death penalty in the state of New York, a man is only sentenced to more time and restrictions if he commits another crime inside a prison. I knew from my background as a deputy sheriff that men who had killed once could easily kill again. I also knew that the Gospel was a threat to those men and that the forces of darkness wanted to snuff out the light that had been shed in that prison.

    As I walked, I looked ahead in the hallway and saw a large man coming my way. I was familiar with this man because he was somewhat of a legend in the prison and I knew him well. His nickname was "The Ox." The Ox had the distinction of being the strongest man in the entire Attica Prison. He was serving two life terms and was noted for his meanness and brute strength. His heavily muscled body was a result of hours of weight lifting and training in the prison weight rooms. I knew from his background that he had the respect of every man in the prison. I found out that at one time he hit a man so hard in his jaw that it snapped the man's collar bone. But, praise God, this man was cordial to me. In a loud, boisterous voice he shouted, "Preacher, come over here!" As I walked over, he looked me over; and with a smirk on his face, announced that the word was out throughout the prison, "They are going to kill you! Someone has made a knife in the metal shop and they are going to stick you with it during the service."

As I heard those words, my heart sank even more. Now it was apparent, it was my time to face death. Inside my heart, I wanted to run. I thought of turning back and walking out the front door. I was under no obligation to give my life. This was merely a contract position of preaching Sunday morning every week. I knew physically it didn't require my life, but spiritually, God was requiring commitment on my part.

I turned to the Ox and, through nervous lips, stammered, "Ox, I'm not going to turn and run. If God has called me to be the chaplain of this prison, then He is going to take care of me. He always has."

I started walking toward the chapel. I heard the Ox say, "Wait up, Preacher." We walked together toward the chapel. I found it strange that he would even walk with me, we seemed so different. He touched my arm and we stopped and he said, "Preacher, I can't sing and I don't know much about religion, but I like you. I like your stuff. If you'll let me pick out five other men from the weight room this morning, we'll be your ushers and we'll help you in the church service!"

God had truly sent me an angel. Unlike a small, dainty cherub, God had given me a three hundred pound powerhouse of a man that had the respect of every inmate inside that prison. Later, I found out that Ox, as a young boy, had a praying mother.

As I approached the auditorium, I shared with the guard my desire to use prison inmates as ushers. He informed me that since the prison was built in 1932, the chapel service had never used inmates as ushers. I insisted that this was the first day of a new beginning. After receiving permission from the warden of the prison, I was told that the inmates could usher the men to the back of the auditorium, and from the back of the auditorium each man who was reprimanded would be given one week of "keep-lock." Keep-lock is restriction to your cell as a form of punishment.

As I waited for the men to come, I began to pray. As the men began to file in to the service, they began to make obscene gestures. It was the largest group of men I had ever seen. I knew that the word had passed through the prison that they were going to kill the ex-deputy sheriff today during the service, and I wondered how many came just to see me die. The noise was thundering. Fear attempted to grip me several times, but I knew that I had to stand and see the salvation of the Lord.

I went to the microphone one more time and turned it up to the feedback squeal. Finally getting their attention, I asked Ox and the five men that he had summoned to come to the front of the auditorium. Instead of looking like church ushers, they appeared to be more of a street gang, built like football players, looking for a chance to use their well-developed muscles. Again I said to the men, "Men, my name is Reverend Wright. I am your new Protestant Chaplain. As I said last week, there is going to be no more dressing up like girls. The bathroom is going to be locked.

No more dirty magazines, and no more cigarettes during the service. When we stand up to sing, we all stand up; when we bow our heads to pray, we all pray. I am going to enforce these regulations with my new ushers. You might recognize my new head usher. His name is "The Ox."Ox waved his hands and a hush fell over the congregation. I continued, "And, as you see, these are his assistants. You may recognize them. You will be warned the first time, and the second time, you will be assisted to the back of the auditorium where you will receive a week's keeplock." An angry murmur came over the crowd.

With great excitement, I preached a sermon on Jesus clearing the temple of the money changers. As I preached, I noticed Ox and his assistants clearing the congregation of troublemakers. It was a somewhat hilarious sight to watch these huge men literally drag offenders from the congregation. It was like no other church service I had ever been in before. Many, many men were dragged to the back of the auditorium where the guards accompanied them back to their cells. I knew that surely God was moving in a way that these men could understand. I know to many who read this book, it will sound like extreme violence, but I am reminded of what Paul said when he spoke to the Romans, he spoke as a Roman. God wanted to deal with these men in a way that prison inmates could understand, and surely He was doing this.

Following the service, I sat with Ox in the front of the auditorium and shared with him the simple salvation plan. And, as we prayed, this huge man accepted Jesus Christ as his personal Savior. Ox, at one time a paid killer, a brutal murderer, would in the future be used in a mighty way to bring revival to Attica Prison.

A MATTER OF COLOR

Ox, once converted, became a catalyst in the revival inside Attica Prison. It was soon apparent that Christians were no longer going to hide their relationship with Jesus. Men began to openly carry their Bibles across the prison yard. Other inmates began to meet in small Bible studies during the yard times. Often at night, a group of men would gather around one cell area where they would study the Bible and pray for the needs of our growing church body. Ox was a different man. Oftentimes, he was approached by troublemakers wanting to know why he would serve a "white man's religion." One night he was cornered in the bathroom by three black Muslims. He would not back down from his faith. They challenged him by saying, "Why are you helping that white chaplain?" They began to call me names. Ox quickly came to my defense and threatened to fight all three. With great wisdom, they retreated. Many times the inmates who were Christians were tempted to use violence. I strongly encouraged them to live in the new man and to reject the old man. For many, this was very difficult. Violence had become a way of life. It was the only way they knew how to communicate.

We formed a deacon board comprised of seven inmates to oversee the affairs of our inmate church. I feel the most successful approach to prison chaplaincy is the concept of the inmate church. For many years, the chaplains have been the one-man program for the entire prison. As in an outside church, it takes a plurality of leadership to make an effective church. As Paul spoke in Corinthians, there are many members to one body. Men inside a prison need to be used so that they may grow in the faith. I began to delegate authority to different inmates. I appointed one man to be the music director. He was responsible for the inmate choir and the music that backed them up. There was choir practice twice weekly with an average attendance of 20 to 30 men. Many times on Sundays, tears would come to my eyes as I heard a special anointing upon those voices. Also, those on the leadership board worked with me to lead worship and to read special scripture readings. The result was a growing, thriving inmate church. Many times, visitors from the outside would remark that their church did not have the enthusiasm and anointing that ours did behind those grey prison walls.

One Sunday morning as I came into the prison and was talking to several of the men prior to the morning service, I heard them say that they were sending a petition to the State Capitol in Albany asking that I would be made the permanent chaplain. I really didn't think much about it. In the prison, petitions were circulated frequently on a large variety of matters. It seemed to be the only way they could make their voices heard, especially when they had a large number who was in agreement on one fact. At that time, I felt it best to neither encourage nor discourage it.

It was by letter that I received a request to come to Albany to meet with Dr. Earl Moore, Director of Chaplains of the New York State Corrections Department.

I drove to the airport and flew the short trip from Rochester to Albany. I was met at the airport by Dr. Moore's assistant, who was very surprised and confused when he met me. He asked me several times if I was Reverend Wright. Later, I would find out why he was confused. Upon entering Dr. Moore's office, his first comment was, "You are white!" I realized that they thought all this time that I was a black minister and had no realization that I was white. On his desk, lay a pile of papers the inmates had sent him from Attica. The petition was signed by twelve hundred inmates! (Ox must have taken the list around!) The petition was worded in this way: "We are writing you to demand that Reverend Robin G. Wright be made the Protestant Chaplain of Attica Prison."After we had talked for several minutes, Dr. Moore confessed that he really desired a black chaplain in the prison and he didn't feel a white chaplain could identify with the black man's problems. Although he was a very religious and educated man, I knew that he didn't really know what God could do through His Holy Spirit. Truly, the Lord had united these men with me in a way that was unexplainable. In the natural eye, it was very strange to see a communion between a white ex-deputy sheriff and a predominately black group of prison inmates, but our God is a God of the supernatural. I knew from that time on that it would be hard to communicate with Dr. Moore on a spiritual level, and after I prayed I put the matter in God's hands and decided to trust Him.

When I left the office that day in Albany, I had been appointed the Protestant Chaplain of the Attica Correctional Facility. I was appointed Protestant Chaplain in 1975. I am the only chaplain ever to be picked by the inmates. I know this was truly a miracle from God; and the Lord, in His great mercy, heard the prayers of those men in Attica Prison.

Life inside the big prison had many challenges, to say the least. As I settled into my new responsibilities, I began to spend time in the chaplain's office. In a big maximum security prison, the inmates fill out request forms for permission to see their chaplain. These forms are filled out for many different reasons: a personal phone call, counseling, and a number of reasons. I soon found that the work load was staggering. With a population of over 1800 inmates, it seemed impossible for one Protestant Chaplain to meet the task. Besides the office counseling, I also tried to see the men in their work areas. Many of the Thursday night Bible study men worked in the factory making school lockers. A complete factory was in operation inside the prison walls. The men punched in and out and had regular breaks, just like workers do in an outside factory. This develops good work skills and teaches them to work responsibly. I had many good times of fellowship with the men when I saw them in their work places or in the prison yard.

Other responsibilities were not quite so pleasant, however. One day I was called to the warden's office early in the morning. The warden shared with me that one young man who was in the prison hospital had died, and that his family in New York City did not want his body, nor would they pay for the shipping of his body back to New York. He wanted me to conduct some kind of service as the man was buried in the prison yard. One of the sergeants drove me to a small plot of land at the rear of the prison. On the plot of land there are approximately fifty small markers, which mark the graves of unclaimed bodies.

There, around a hole in the earth, stood six men who had just finished digging a grave by hand. I looked at the naked body in the clear plastic bag and realized how little life meant to many people. I didn't know this man. I knew his name, but I did not know him. I began to see the reality of prison life. Many of the men and women that are in prison today have been cut off by their families, forgotten, and written off as unchangeable. I knew that Jesus Christ and a relationship with Him was the only tangible form of rehabilitation for men in prison. I knew that when the world gave up on men, Jesus never did.

Another difficult time for me as chaplain was when I had to give out death notices to men who were inmates. These were usually a notification of the death of a next of kin. One day, I received a phone call from the warden's office notifying me that my head deacon's son had been killed with a pistol shot to the head in Harlem. I immediately put a call out for him and began to pray how I would share this tragedy with a man I had grown to love so much. When I first came to the prison, John, along with several others, helped me to learn my way through the large facility.

His kindness and encouragement had been very helpful to me. A sincere man with a strong Christian faith, he was an inspiration to many. He was in prison on a short term, soon to be released. We prayed many times for his family, and especially his son. The son had been killed in a hold-up. He was not involved, he was simply an innocent by-stander. My mind raced, as I prayed, concerning how I would share this death with my friend. He was soon at the door, and I guided him into the inner office. Before I was able to speak, the tears welled in my eyes and I began to weep. He knew what I was going to say before I even spoke the words. He said, "My son is dead, isn't he?" I answered, "He is dead, John." We clasped our hands together and both wept bitter tears. Following a time of praying, I walked with John back to his cell encouraging him in every way I could. Men who are in prison, especially maximum security, are not allowed to go home in most cases. I felt, with my Christian brother John, his great anguish of not being able to spend those last minutes with his son. I would repeat this task of sharing death notices many times. It never became easier.

THE MINISTRY GROWS

One morning as I entered the front gate, the guard on duty informed me that the warden wanted to see me immediately. In his office, Warden Smith shared with me that reporters from the local television station in Rochester, New York wanted to visit the prison on the sixth anniversary of the famous riots. Attica Prison is known throughout the U.S. for the terrible, violent acts committed during the 1971 riots. A number of inmates overtook the guards and held them hostage for seven days. When the State Troopers, under the order of the Governor of the state of New York, retook the prison, 46 men were killed in a seventeen second period. It is one of the most infamous riots ever held in prison history. The local CBS affiliate, Channel 10 in Rochester, wanted to capitalize on the notoriety of the anniversary of these riots.

Mr. Smith, the prison warden, knew of the great things that were happening in the Thursday night Bible study and felt that Attica needed some good publicity, instead of the bad publicity it usually received. He asked me if I would consider having a camera crew film the 2 1/2 hour Thursday night Bible study. At first I was reluctant, but felt that I could be of service to him in showing how God was changing men from crime to Christ. Also, I felt it would be a terrific witness for Christ, showing the rehabilitation and regeneration that comes from a Christ-centered life. We made the final agreements and I was to meet the film crew on the following Thursday night.

As I drove into the prison that night, I was amazed to see three men and a reporter loaded down with film equipment and power packs and all the video equipment needed to film our Bible study. Several of the men that usually came along with me to the prison were with me, as well; and we had prayed and fasted that day concerning the meeting. It was our desire that Jesus be lifted up and that nothing would be twisted or turned around to lift up man.

That night was one of the greatest meetings we ever had. Over 175 men came to Bible study. There was special music, our church choir sang, and, following the service, the reporter interviewed several of the inmates. In these many interviews, the men shared how important this time of fellowship in Christ was. One man shared that he had never been to church on the outside, but would never miss one of these Thursday night studies.

Following the service, as we walked to the front door, the reporter and camera crew shared with me how greatly moved they were by the service. They shared the fear they had as they entered the prison and how it had evaporated as they met these wonderful Christian men. One man shared with me that he would never forget that Bible study in Attica Prison.

We watched the following day as a short, two minute report was given on Channel 10 in Rochester. We were well-satisfied that it lifted up Jesus and the reporter proclaimed, "Where there once was riot, there is now revival!" We thought that would be the end of the broadcast, and did not expect anything more.

It was the following week, however, that we began to receive phone calls and letters from all over the United States. To our surprise, the local CBS affiliate gave their tape to the CBS Nightly News, and it was aired as the final segment of a nightly broadcast. People from all over the United States reported seeing how God was moving inside Attica Prison.

Soon I began to receive speaking engagements from all over the U.S. I began to speak at many Full Gospel Business Men's Fellowship International meetings and in churches of every denomination. Everyone wanted to hear of what God was doing inside the famous Attica Prison. Not only did I have the opportunity to share with Christian organizations, but also with civic organizations, such as the Lion's Club and others. It was truly a chance to testify to what God was doing inside of Attica Prison.

THE STORY OF STEVE

While serving in the prison, I had many interesting experiences. One of my favorites was the story of a young man named Steve. The Thursday night Bible study in the prison chapel was so dynamic that many inmates came just to watch. One of those inmates was Steve. The first night he came, he sat in the last row in the farthest section of the auditorium. He didn't participate in any way except to listen. When I attempted to get him involved, he resisted and simply said, "I just want to watch and listen." This young man in his twenties was hurting badly, but was unable to ask for help. A lifetime of hurt and pain was reflected in his face. Immediately, I became burdened for him and sent several of my strongest Christian brothers to speak to him. He rejected anyone who attempted to show him the love of the Lord. The more I saw him, the more I was burdened.

One day I went to the records department in the administrative section of the prison. I was on a mission. I needed to know more about Steve. What caused this young man all this terrible bitterness and rejection? I had never looked into any of the inmates personal files before. I didn't want the crimes they committed to persuade me in any way. I was not there to judge the men, but to help and encourage them through the ministry of the Gospel. Their past, to me, was not as important as their future. God has a wonderful plan and purpose for everyone, even for those who were not accepted by society for the mistakes they made. I am always encouraged to know that the first man in Paradise after Calvary was the thief who hung on the cross next to Jesus.

When I read Steve's file I was saddened, to say the least. When he was seven years old he was molested by his own father. After being moved to another family member's home, he was misused again. This happened several times. Finally placed in a foster home, he rebelled and went to a youth detention center; then, at age nineteen, he held up a local corner store with a rusted gun that wouldn't shoot. He got a mere forty-five dollars and seven years in Attica Prison for armed robbery. When I looked at his correspondence list, I was amazed. No one wrote Steve. On top of that, he never had even one visitor. Even in the prison there is a class system. Those who have no visitors or letters are considered "losers." But in God's kingdom there are no "losers," only "winners." Now my burden for Steve became a crusade; I had to help this man, or he had no hope or future.

One Sunday, while speaking in a local church in the Rochester, New York area, an older couple, Mr. and Mrs. Richards, approached me after the service. They were retired and wanted to be involved in some type of prison ministry. Mrs. Richards said, "Even if we could just visit a lonely inmate, it would be a blessing for us to help." It was as though a light bulb lit up over my head. Steve! The Lord had answered my prayers. It just wasn't how I thought it would happen. Now I had to set things up.

THE STORY OF STEVE

On Monday I walked to Steve's cell. I told Steve that I had an older couple that wanted to visit him. He was reluctant, and informed me that no one loved or cared for him. I told him that Jesus loved him, and again asked if he would allow the Richards' to visit. He begrudgingly said, "Okay." I called the Richards' and asked them to meet me at the front gate on Saturday morning. In the meantime, I did the paperwork necessary for them to visit.

When they arrived that Saturday, they came prepared. Mr. Richards had a beautiful brand-new Bible with Steve's name imprinted on the front, and Mrs. Richards had baked a tin of warm, homemade chocolate chip cookies. After going through the metal detectors, they followed me to the Visitors Room.

Steve was called out of the cell and came down to the Visitors Room. He was a mess! He hadn't shaved or even combed his hair. He had no personal pride and it showed. It was an awkward first meeting but the Richards' greeted him like a long lost son. God's unconditional love is unstoppable.

After the visit, I approached Steve. He was dumbfounded. He couldn't understand why two

Christian people would spend time with him. After all, they had a son who was a doctor and a daughter who was married to a missionary. Yet they embraced Steve with a love and kindness he had never experienced. He agreed to see them again.

They visited Steve every Saturday without fail. They brought cookies, tracts, and a loving kindness that would melt the toughest heart. I would pass by the visiting room and see them sharing the Bible with Steve. Slowly, he began to change. The Saturday visits were the highlight of his life. He began to comb his hair and shine his shoes, and his hardened heart began to soften. He had a reason to live.

One Sunday, after entering the front gate and walking toward the chapel, I heard someone yell my name. As I turned, I saw Steve running toward me. He had a glow about him that I had never seen before. He said, "Chaplain, I'm coming to church today, and from now on I'll be at every service. Yesterday 'Mom and Dad' Richards led me to Christ." The unconditional love of two people had changed a man full of hate into one of the best Christian men in the prison. He became an elder in our prison church system and began Bible correspondence courses.

The Richards introduced Steve to a young woman they knew in their church. This precious young mother had a little girl that she was raising as a single mom. They needed a husband and father and Steve needed a family to love and support him. I married them one Sunday afternoon in the prison chapel with the Richards as their witnesses. The entire prison church attended.

Later, Steve was paroled and began a new life with his wife and daughter. He opened a restaurant in the North Chili, New York area; and eventually he became the president of the Full Gospel Business Men's Fellowship Chapter there. This man that was so hurt and rejected in his life was transformed by two people that decided to love him unconditionally.

I have shared Steve's story many times over the years, and many lives have been touched by this wonderful testimony.

THE BUM STORY

The radio ministry was growing rapidly, and we were now on every Saturday morning on six different stations. During the program "From the Chaplain's Desk," we interviewed men and women who were changed from crime to Christ. We also interviewed law enforcement officers, prison guards, and others who could testify to the fact that men could be changed by a living relationship with Jesus Christ.

Our radio testimonies were reaching many people throughout the U.S, and I found it difficult many times to keep up the mail and cards that needed to be answered. We were also sending Bibles and books to men in smaller facilities that did not have chaplains. All in all, it was an expensive and time-consuming operation.

THE BUM STORY

I found that some churches cared, but many others simply did not find a heart for prisoners. Many considered missions as only helping those in other countries. I wanted to share with them in words, if possible, the need to minister to those in our own community. At that time in New York state, there were over 30,000 men and women incarcerated. Three out of every five came back to prison. During 1975, it cost $10,000 to $15,000 to house an inmate. Why couldn't churches recognize the prison ministry as a mission? It was so easy to recognize Africa and India and all the foreign countries, but not those who were lost in our country.

I prayed sincerely over this matter seeking the Spirit of God and the Spirit's leading. It was during that night that God spoke to me a story that I wrote. For lack of a better name, I entitled it "The Bum Story." I knew it didn't come from me because when I sat down to write it, it flowed through me in a way that I knew could come only from the Spirit of God. I shared it the following Saturday on my radio broadcast, and soon people began to ask for copies of it. One dear woman sent us a check to cover the cost of printing 40,000 tracts. Since that time, we have produced over 400,000 copies of the tract; it has been published in magazines and periodicals across the U.S. Here is the story:

It was a beautiful, sunny Sunday morning as the derelict awoke next to the garbage can in the alley. He took a good look at himself. He was a mess! His old, tattered suit was full of holes and newspapers wrapped around his shoes. He hadn't shaved in months and his hair was stiff with the dirt of the street. He was filthy and dirty. He had not eaten a decent meal in weeks, and the smell of human vomit and garbage filled the alley.

As he stood to his feet, something caught his eye. It was the shiny, white cross on the steeple of a church several blocks away. "I'm sick of the way I'm living," he said to himself. "Today I'm going to start my life over again, and I know the Lord will forgive me." He brushed himself off and started walking towards that bright cross.

As he walked closer to the church, he heard the bells ringing, and he became excited with the thought of a new life in Christ. His heart pounded quickly as

THE BUM STORY

he saw the big stained glass windows and heard the organ's soft tones. His step became faster as he saw the big cars and the women with their fine furs escorted by men in expensive suits.

As he walked to the steps leading up to the open doors, he pulled himself up to his full height and said, "Praise God, today I can start my life over again." As he started up the steps to the church, two big ushers grabbed him and <u>threw him down the stairs</u>! He picked himself up and started up the stairs. The same two ushers threw him down the stairs again, and one yelled, "GET OUT OF HERE YOU ROTTEN, STINKING BUM. GO BACK TO THE GHETTO WHERE YOU BELONG!!"

He was crushed. He turned away from the church and walked towards the ghetto. His shoulders slumped, the tears filled his eyes. They rolled down his cheeks and fell on his coat. "Why, Lord, why," he cried. "They just wouldn't let me in that church, Lord! Why wouldn't they let me in?" Suddenly, he felt the presence of the Holy Spirit and a voice said, "Don't worry, son, I can't get in either!"

The church that I am talking about in this story

is not the church physically, as much as it is the church in our hearts. I was trying to share with people that our churches are not showcases for saints, but hospitals for sick sinners; and that as Christians, we must love those who are lost and reach out to them in love-Jesus-type love. Jesus said in John 6:37, "All that the Father giveth me shall come to me; and him that cometh to me I will in no wise cast out."

    I knew this was the story that I needed. I knew it was a story that would reach people when my own words wouldn't. I knew it was truly given from the Spirit of God. I shared that story over the years many times. I believe God gave it as a special way to reach people and to soften hardened hearts. I knew God wanted to bless His men in prison in a way they had never known.

    The notoriety was also good as it opened the door for many other Christian ministries to come into Attica Prison. We especially wanted to have Chaplain Ray Hoekstra of the International Prison Ministry in Dallas, Texas to come. Ever since we started in the prison ministry, Chaplain Ray had been faithful in sending Bibles, books, and greeting cards to the prison whenever we needed them. He published the magazine "Prison Evangelism" and his daily broadcast, "Cellblock," reached over three hundred prisons across the country. Of all the prison ministries in operation today, Chaplain Ray had the best known ministry among the inmates. His faithfulness and kindness to them over the years had made him a legend to the men. We felt it was very important for him to come and visit the men inside this prison.

When I notified him, he was very excited about coming. He also asked Cookie Rodriguez, former gang member and author of the book, "Please Make Me Cry," to come as well. Cookie ran a home for girls, and brought her all-girl choir to minister.

On Saturday morning, I took Chaplain Ray, his wife, Leola, Cookie, and all the girls on a tour through the prison. They were more than surprised at the response they received.

On Saturday afternoon, we invited the entire population of the prison to a special Gospel service. Over 700 men filled the auditorium. I knew that the main reason many of the men came was because of the fourteen pretty young women that would be singing. When the girls finished singing, Cookie Rodriguez, with her broken Puerto Rican accent, confronted the men this way, "Many of you men came down to look at the pretty girls, but while you are looking at the pretty girls, God is looking at your heart!"

She went on to share her testimony of being a prostitute and of being one of the street people that was changed by the ministry of Reverend David Wilkerson and the Teen Challenge Street Ministry. She told how she had come from a tough street life, addicted to drugs, to a minister now sharing her experience with others and helping young girls to begin new lives. When she finished her sermon, she gave a frank altar call. Over 150 men, many with tears in their eyes, came forward to accept Jesus Christ as their personal Savior. It was one of the most moving services I had ever been in, and truly, the Holy Spirit had descended in a very special way.

After that visit, Chaplain Ray came back to film the movie "God's Prison Gang." Also, we had many other Christian ministries come and minister to the men. Charles Colson, Nancy Honeytree, the Gospel Echoes, and many others, including local church groups came to share in the revival at Attica Prison.

As the numbers grew in our services, we also knew that our ministry must grow. It was during this time that the state appointed another Protestant Chaplain, Reverend Jeff Carter, a black minister from Buffalo, New York. Jeff didn't have any prison experience, but was very strong in counseling and administration. He began to do much of the counseling and administrative work, and I concentrated on the services and evangelistic meetings.

There was a need at this time to see men water baptized. The prison had never had a water baptismal tank in all the years it had existed. I spoke to the warden concerning buying a tank and he told me there were no funds available. He also told me we should be able to sprinkle the men, and that would be sufficient. I shared with him the importance of water baptism to our Christian beliefs. Finally, he consented that we could have a water baptismal tank as long as the prison wasn't going to pay for it.

Approximately thirty days later, as I entered the prison one morning, I was stopped by a guard who said that the warden wanted to see me immediately, even before I went to my office. I knew by the tone of the guard's voice that I was in trouble with the warden. As I entered the warden's secretary's office, she raised her eyebrows in such a way that I knew I was entering the "lion's den." Warden Smith and I had become friends, but I knew that on certain issues he was immovable. He truly had a heart for the men, but had to maintain maximum security and discipline.

As I walked into the inner office, he threw a piece of paper at me. It was a C.O.D. invoice for a water baptismal tank that I ordered. When I ordered the tank, which was built by a Christian organization and given free as a gift to prisons, I never realized I would be responsible for the shipping fee. There, on the floor, was the bill for over $200 for shipping. Warden Smith was irate and voiced his anger with me. I knew that it was a time for me to be still and allow him to express his feelings. I grew to respect this man greatly, and found him to be a man of great wisdom. The water baptismal tank was worth all we went through to get it. Later that year, over 100 men would be baptized in a special service. For the first time in over 35 years men were being baptized by immersion in Attica Prison.

AN INVITATION TO AFRICA

It was July of 1979 that I received a letter from Reverend Chaplain David Muchui, Provincial Prison's Chaplain, Central Province, Nyeri, Kenya, East Africa. In the letter that I received, he shared his concern for the prisoners that were under his supervision in the East African prisons. He had received my name from the Logos International Prison Ministry Directory. He wrote for advice and help in the prison chaplaincy. The letter was beautiful, and I felt a spirit of unity between us. We began to correspond on a regular basis, and I began to enclose material I thought would be helpful in the ministry for him there in East Africa. In one letter, he asked if I could come and tour the prisons and work with him.

I prayed over this matter and asked the Lord for confirmation. The confirmation came a short while later. One night while I was at the Elim Bible Institute in Lima, New York, I was approached by Reverend Simeon Obayo. Brother Obayo was the District Elder for the Pentecostal Evangelical Fellowships of Africa (P.E.F.A.). He shared that the Lord told him that I was to speak at his churches in Keyna, Africa as his guest. Praise the Lord! He gave me the confirmation that I needed. I knew now that it was God that had desired for me to go, and He would open the doors.

    I wrote a letter to all those whom I knew had a concern in this ministry: those who worked with me in the Attica Prison revival, those who had been affected by our ministry in local jails and prisons, and even to a large number of ex-inmates who were now functioning as civilians on the outside. I shared with them my need of going to Africa and ministering in the prisons there. The result was overwhelming. Within thirty days $4,600 came in through the mail for the ministry. God was truly opening the doors now for the prison ministry to go to Africa.

I still felt as though I needed confirmation from the head of all the prisons in Kenya, East Africa. I knew from experience that in order to work effectively in prison ministry, God wants his ministers to completely submit to the authority in the institutions they visit. I've learned over the years that we are subject, as Christians, to authority; and God honors those ministers who are in order as they enter prisons. It was within two weeks that my confirmation came. I received a letter from Reverend Doctor Nigeri. Dr. Nigeri was the head chaplain of all the prisons in Kenya, East Africa. In his letter he asked if I would come and tour the prisons and lead workshops with the chaplains of all those prisons. I was thrilled at the request and wrote a quick letter back confirming my visit.

After a long plane ride by way of London, England, I arrived in Africa. The airport in Nairobi was quite different than I had expected. Nairobi is the capital of Kenya and, in many respects, a modern type city. There to meet me was both the Senior Chaplain and the Regional Chaplain. After a time of fellowship and food, we mapped out our plan for the next five weeks. The schedule was heavy, and we all shared the great anticipation of what God was going to do.

Africa's prisons are so different from American prisons. Conditions are poor, sickness abounds, and most of the men are hopeless in their situation. As I prayed asking the Lord to direct me, I felt as though the message He would have me preach would be one of love. Probably one of the most effective words to share with men in prison is love. When a person doesn't know love, he doesn't know self-worth. When he loses love, he loses respect, for not only others, but for himself. Jesus came as a love gift from God. If we can share with people the love that is in Christ, they can have hope. I knew that I was on a mission of love. The reason God sent me to Africa was to tell these people in prison that God loved them. The next thirty-one days would be hectic. Many times I would be exhausted to the point of wondering if I could even preach, but the Lord was sufficient in giving me strength.

The first service we held was at the Nyeri main prison right outside Nairobi. This would be my first service in an African prison, and was a new experience for me. In most of our prison services in the U.S., we hold the service in either the chapel or the prison auditorium. There is a time of worship and singing, and usually we close with a message and an altar call. In the African prisons there are no auditoriums or chapels, and most of all the services are held in the open air yard of the prison.

As we walked into the first prison in Nyeri, we saw in the middle of the yard area three chairs. I was informed that those were the three chairs we were to sit in, and that we were to sit down. The Senior Chaplain, the District Chaplain, and I sat in the chairs awaiting the arrival of the inmates.

Soon the entire prison population was brought into the yard area. This was a new experience for me, unlike anything I had ever seen before. Over 700 inmates dressed in white shorts and white shirts were brought from wherever they were into the yard area. Everyone had to attend. There were no exceptions. People were brought from the hospital area and from every conceivable area of the prison into the yard.

They surrounded us as they knelt and sat down.

There was no noise. No one was allowed to speak. They were the most subdued, obedient prisoners I had ever met. I found out later the reason why. Because of sickness and poor diet they had lost their strength. They were not even strong enough to be noisy or unruly. They had been brought to a place whereby they had lost their self will. Their strength had been sapped.

The Senior Chaplain stood to his feet and began to speak in Kiswahili. About sixty percent of all the prisoners in Kenya can read and write English. The national language is Kiswahili which is understood by almost everyone. We felt it best for me to preach and be interpreted in the native language of Kiswahili.

Following an introduction and comments by the Senior Chaplain, the Regional Chaplain stood to his feet and began to sing a few choruses. I was surprised to see most of the men join in.

After that time he introduced me, and I stood to my feet. It was an awesome feeling to look over 700 men assembled in one courtyard. I was the only white person there, and I didn't know their language.

I knew I was a foreigner, and I knew that most of the Africans have very little to do with white people because of the English background of Kenya, a country that revolted to receive its independence from Great Britain.

I had never preached through an interpreter, and I knew that I must keep my sentences short and to the point. I also knew that I couldn't use slang words that were slang words back in America. They had to be words that could be translated into Kiswahili. I began to share the simple story of Jesus on the cross and the two thieves who hung with him. I shared of the rebellion of one thief and the acceptance of the other. I knew that they knew the word "remember" as the thief said, "Lord, remember me when thou comest into thy kingdom." Men in prison have to remember: families, loved ones, and living in the outside world. I knew that many men spent much of their time in prison remembering the things they once had. I shared simply with them how the thief asked Jesus to remember him, and Jesus, through great grace and mercy said, "Today you will be with me in paradise." As I shared this simple story of love and how much Jesus loved them and gave the altar call, over three hundred fifty men stood to their feet to accept Jesus as their personal Savior.

Before coming to Africa, I had received a commitment from Chaplain Ray of the International Prison Ministry in Dallas, Texas, to give each man saved during these African crusades a brand new Bible, reference material, and life-changing books. When I had talked to him previously, I had never realized that during these African crusades over 1,760 inmates would make first time commitments to Jesus Christ as their personal Savior. I was told later by the government officials, as I was leaving to come home, that this was the first time an American evangelist was allowed to give crusades in the Kenya prisons. I was also told that never before had this many inmates made decisions to accept Christ. I knew that it was only through the Lord Jesus Christ that we could see such results.

In the weeks to come, we would minister in prisons at a hectic pace. Sometimes we would do two prisons and a church in one day. Many times I would feel close to exhaustion, but supernaturally

God would give me new strength.

Probably the greatest personal experience for me on the trip was my visit to the prison in Mombasa. The prison there is well-know throughout Kenya. It is a prison halfway between Mombasa on the coast of Kenya and the capitol city of Nairobi. The prison is surrounded by a large, high chain fence. I thought at first when we came to the prison that the fence was to keep the inmates in, but I found out later that it was built for the purpose of keeping wild elephants and rhinoceros out of the garden that the prisoners maintained for their food. The prison didn't really need a fence to keep men in because of its location in the middle of the Kenya plains. If a man was to escape, it was very unlikely that he would live to reach any population.

I had heard much about this prison. It is probably the most notorious prison in the continent of Africa. The reason for its notoriety is that only killers and murderers are sent to this prison. It is one of the few prisons in Kenya that is guarded by men from the Zulu tribe. Zulu warriors are the most feared and respected throughout Africa. They average between six foot five to seven feet tall and weigh between 250 to 300 pounds. Their fierce loyalty and incredible size make them the perfect guards for this type of prison

Prior to the service, we were escorted to one of the administration buildings. While we were in the building, one of these guards came to visit us. He shared that he, too, was a Christian and loved Jesus Christ. He had heard of us coming. I found out his name was John. He had four children and lived in the compound area with the other guards. They had been praying for revival inside this prison, and prayed that God would use us in a mighty way. He warned me again, however, of the intensity of the atmosphere inside this prison.

Most of the men in this prison were the most violent in all Africa. I knew of their hatred of the white man. The stage was set for a confrontation, but I knew that what the devil meant for evil, God could use for good.

Finally, it came time for the outdoor meeting. The men were not asked if they wanted to come. They were simply herded into the yard like cattle.

We were seated in the traditional seating area in the center of the compound. I looked to the gun towers around me and noticed John's friendly wave from the corner tower. It gave me a sense of security in the middle of a frightening situation.

Soon the men began to file in. The looks and stares from these men were frightening. I sensed the anger, hatred, and violence that they felt for me. As the song leader attempted to lead the songs in Kiswahili, I noticed a resistance of the majority of the men. Many felt angry that they had to even be there. I felt a chill of fear attempt to grip me. Here I was the only white man in the middle of the most violent prison in all of Kenya.

I knew that I couldn't address these men with any fear in my heart. As they were leading the song service, I bowed my head and began pray, "Lord, you saved my life in Vietnam, you saved me from death in Attica Prison. Surely you brought me to Africa, since you opened the doors in a way I could never conceive. Father, into your hands I commit my spirit. Please help me to overcome this fear".

AN INVITATION TO AFRICA

    Suddenly, I felt the peace of God that passes all understanding flood my soul, and from the corner of my eye I caught a glimpse of two guards standing behind me. Without looking at them, I knew they must have been Zulu. They were very, very tall and very, very large standing directly behind me to the right. As the chaplain introduced me, I stood to my feet and preached concerning the love of Jesus. It was a special word, and I knew the Holy Spirit had anointed it. At the altar call over 300 men accepted Christ. Many of the men came forward with tears in their eyes. It was one of the most anointed meetings I had ever been in. The Spirit of God fell in a most magnificent way.

    After the men began to file out back to their work places, I wanted to thank the two guards that were behind me. As I turned, I saw no guards at all. I looked again and saw nothing but a sea of inmates. Following the service, the large guard, John, came down from the tower; and I questioned him concerning what happened. "John, I was very concerned for my life, but I felt great peace when

I saw those two large guards behind me." John answered, "I too was concerned for you Reverend Wright; and I prayed that God would give you strength, but I want you to know that there were no guards behind you, only the guards in the gun towers."

I knew the Lord had sent two angels for my protection. John and I began to laugh. We knew that God was faithful in hearing the prayers of the people who had prayed for that prison. In the midst of a volatile situation God sent his very own to maintain the peace. I shall never forget my angel visitation, and I knew truly the peace that comes from being united with God in the Spirit.

The rest of my tour of Africa took me throughout the eastern Kenya area. Besides the many prisons I ministered in, I was also able to share in several churches and to lead a two-day workshop for all the chaplains in East Africa. In these workshops I shared with them my vision for the ultimate inmate church, the concept of inmates in leadership positions maintaining the church and its functions.

I left Africa thankful for the many opportunities to minister God's word, but most of all, to be able to share some of the prison chaplaincy principles that we had been applying in Attica Prison. God's word and spiritual principles are applicable anywhere.

SAYING GOOD-BYE

I knew my days as Chaplain of Attica Prison were numbered. The Department of Corrections in Albany, New York, had begun to replace white chaplains with black chaplains. They felt because of the large number of black inmates that a black chaplain could better identify with the problems of black inmates. I knew that this wasn't true because I knew that in Christ there are no colors.

It was during this time that God began to show me that my work at Attica Prison was only for a season. It had been a season of planting seeds that would be harvested at a later time. I began to sense in my spirit that God was moving me on in a different direction.

The men, however, felt quite differently about

it. They sensed that soon I would no longer be their chaplain. It was always amazing to me how inmates would find out about important issues before they were even announced to those in places of responsibility. It was as though they had a keen network of spies throughout the entire system.

One night after services, a group of men approached me with a petition in hand. On the petition they wrote that they didn't want a black chaplain. They asked me if they could come to my defense, as they knew I would be asked to leave. I told them that I felt if God wanted me to be there, He would make a way for me. They weren't satisfied with that answer, and demanded that they fight for my position. I asked them to wait as we sought the leadership of the Lord.

Several nights later, I was reading my Bible and God drew my attention through His Holy Spirit to I Kings 3:16. In this account, two women and one baby are brought before King Solomon. He is called to decide which woman is actually the mother of the child. In his great wisdom, he asked for a sword, and as his assistant brings the sword, he gives the order to cut the living child in two and give half to each mother. The real mother was so filled with compassion that she said to King Solomon, "Please, my lord, give her the living baby! Don't kill him!" The other woman said, "Neither I nor you shall have him, cut him in two."After King Solomon had heard this, he knew the real mother. The real mother was willing to give up the child in order that the child might live. As I read this, tears welled in my eyes. I knew that I was being called to give up this "Baby." It was the "Baby" that I saw birthed from a small Bible study to a growing, thriving church. But it was never mine. The Lord had used me to plant, and now He was to use someone else to pastor. It was a difficult pill to swallow, but I truly knew the Lord was speaking to me. The next day this was confirmed through a friend who was given the same scripture. We prayed together that the men would be able to understand that I was no longer going to be their chaplain.

The next Thursday night, following the song service, I shared this story with them. They were shocked. Many of them had never know another pastor. Some argued, some were angry with me, some understood. The drive home that night seemed especially long; and as I drove, my mind drifted over the past four years. It had all begun in a little county jail and ended with the greatest revival Attica Prison ever knew. The bond of love that was built between these men and myself could not be severed by my leaving physically. While my heart was heavy, I knew in my spirit that I was being obedient to God. I would rather give up my chaplaincy and the Bible study, than to see a fight that would do nothing to glorify God. These men needed to be secure in their services. Far above my own personal desires and my pride was the priority of their growth in the Lord. Jesus was calling me to die to self and to put down my own desires.

  The following week I wrote my resignation to the Director of Chaplains and to the warden of the prison. Warden Smith came to my office, and with tears in his eyes, asked me to remain on. He promised to stand behind me and even to fly to Albany in my defense. It gave me a great opportunity to share with him what God had given me. I shook his hand that day for the last time.

As I left the prison I said good-bye to many of the guards I had come to know during the time I had been there. I walked to the parking lot. With one last look, I said good-bye to a portion of my life I will never forget.

ADDENDUM

Much has happened in my life since I originally wrote this book in 1984. After leaving the prison, I began a new church in western New York; and following that, I traveled in the evangelistic field. Over the years I have pioneered several churches and I now pastor a wonderful church in Las Vegas, Nevada. Also, I host a local radio broadcast heard throughout the area.

I heard from many of the inmates when I first left Attica, but have lost touch with most of them through the years. It is a common practice in New York to move the prisoners around in the prison system. It prevents gangs from forming.

While I have ministered in several prisons through the years, most of my ministry these days is involved with my local church. After traveling for so many years, it's nice just to be settled in one place, ministering to the people the Lord has sent me.

When I reviewed this book for reprinting, it brought back many great memories. I laughed and cried, for this story was such a dramatic time in my life. I know when I get to heaven, I will see "The Ox" and the rest of my brothers. Until then, I have the assurance that God did something special in that prison and in my life, as well. Thank you for reading this book.

May God bless you richly,
Pastor Rob Wright

PLAN OF SALVATION

Steps To Receiving Christ As Your Savior

1. **Acknowledge that you are a sinner.**
   For all have sinned, and come short of the glory of God (Romans 3:23).
   All we like sheep have gone astray; we have turned everyone to his own way... (Isaiah 53:6).

2. **Know that you are under the penalty of death.**
   The soul that sinneth, it shall die (Ezekiel 18:4).
   The wages of sin is death (Romans 6:23a).

3. **Jesus has a full pardon for you. - - Accept it.**
   Who forgiveth all thine iniquities (Psalm 103:3).
   For God so loved the world, that He gave His only begotten son, that whosoever believeth in Him should not perish, but have everlasting life (John 3:16).

But God commendeth His love toward us, in that while we were yet sinners, Christ died for us (Romans 5:8).

Wherefore He is able to save them to the uttermost that come unto God by Him... (Hebrews 7:25).

The gift of God is eternal life through Jesus Christ our Lord (Romans 6:23b).

4. **Repent of your sins. Tell God you are sorry.**
Let the wicked forsake his way, and the unrighteous man his thoughts: and let him re turn unto the Lord, and he will have mercy upon him; and to our God, for he will abundantly pardon (Isaiah 55:7).

5. **Do it now!**
Behold, now is the accepted time; behold, now is the day of salvation (2 Corinthians 6:2). Behold, I stand at the door, and knock; if any man hear my voice, and open the door, I will come in to him, and will sup with him, and he with me (Revelation 3:20).

6. **Pray this prayer with me...**
Heavenly Father,
I know that I am a sinner and I ask for Your mercy. I believe Christ died for my sins. I repent of my sins and I ask Your forgiveness. I am willing to turn from my sins and my old way of life and to live for You. I now invite Jesus Christ to come into my heart as my personal Savior. I will follow and obey Christ, by Your grace, making Him the Lord of my life, from this day forward. Amen.

If you have prayed this prayer with me in sincerity and truly believe, then you are now a child of God. Now you can be sure. Because the Bible says so!!!

I (Jesus) am the resurrection, and the life; he that believeth in me, though he were dead, yet shall he live: And whosoever liveth and believeth in me shall never die (John 11:25-26). If we confess our sins, He is faithful and just to forgive us our sins, and to cleanse us from all unrighteousness (1John 1:9).
But as many as received Him, to them gave He power to become the sons of God, even to them that believe on His name (John 1:12).

WELCOME TO GOD'S FAMILY!!!

About the author……

Rob Wright resides in Las Vegas, Nevada, with his wife Julie, and is the founder and Senior Pastor of Abundant Grace Church, an interdenominational Bible-based church.

As an evangelist, Rob has ministered across the United States, Canada, Africa, England, and Haiti. He has spoken at over 460 "Full Gospel Business Men's" meetings, and has appeared on CBN'S "700 Club", Praise the Lord", and "Word of Faith" television programs.

His personal testimony was featured in the June 1987 issue of "Guideposts" magazine, and he has written articles published in "The Pentecostal Evangel", "Christian Life", and "Dove" magazines.

His radio broadcast, "Grace For Today", is heard several times weekly throughout the Las Vegas area.

Address all correspondence to:

Reverend Rob Wright
Post Office Box 33001
Las Vegas, NV 89133-3001
www.graceinlasvegas.com